FIELDS OF LEARNING

FIELDS OF LEARNING

A Retrospect on One-room Schools in Allegany County, New York

William A. Paquette, Ph.D.
History Professor

David A. Dean
Cover Art

New Dominion Press ● Norfolk ● Virginia

Fields of Learning:
A Retrospect on One-room Schools in Allegany County, New York

Published by:

New Dominion Press
New Dominion Media/New Dominion Press
1217 Godfrey Avenue, Norfolk, Virginia 23504-3218
www.NewDominionPress.com

First Printing: October 2019

No part of this book may be reproduced, stored in any information storage or retrieval system, electronic or mechanical, including photocopying, recording or transmission in any form whatsoever, except in the case of short quotations printed in articles or reviews, with attribution and without the written consent of the author, except as provided by the copyright law of the United States of America.

Cover Design, Graphic Design, and Typography by New Dominion Press
Cover Art by David A. Dean

Copyright © 2019 by William A. Paquette
All Rights Reserved.

Publisher's Cataloging-in-Publication Data
provided by Five Rainbows Cataloging Services

Name: Paquette, William A., 1947- author.
Title: Fields of learning: A retrospect on one-room schools in Allegany County, New York / William A. Paquette.
Description: Norfolk, VA : New Dominion Press, 2019. | Includes bibliographical references.
Identifiers: LCCN 2019915148 | ISBN 978-1-733-12921-3 (paperback)
Subjects: LCSH: Rural schools--New York (State). | Education, Rural. | New York (State)--History. | Education--History--19th century. | Architecture in education. | Education--Curricula. | Teachers--Training of. | BISAC: EDUCATION / Rural. | EDUCATION / History. | EDUCATION / Teacher Training & Certification. | ARCHITECTURE / Buildings / Landmarks & Monuments.
Classification: LCC LC5147.N4 P37 2019 (print) | DDC 371.009/747--dc23.

First Edition

Dedication

Jean Milliman

Genesee Township Historian

Jean's leadership and vision led to the acquisition, restoration, and dedication of the Ceres, New York School as a National Historic Site and as a Museum for the BRAG (Bolivar, Allentown, Richburg, and Genesee) Historical Society.

Table of Contents

Preface 1

Chapter One 5
  One-Room Schools: A History, 1869 - 1945

Chapter Two 29
  One-Room Schools: A Photographic Essay

Chapter Three 93
  The High Schools, 1910

Chapter Four 107
  School Consolidation: K–12

Chapter Five 125
  Higher Education in Allegany County

Chapter Six 129
  Surviving One-Room Schools: 2019

Art and Photographic Credits 143

Bibliography 145

About the Contributors 149

PREFACE

My maternal ancestors arrived in the southern half of Allegany County, New York in 1822, and settled in the township of Bolivar. They were descendants of *Mayflower* passenger Edward Fuller who arrived in Plymouth (1620), Thomas Roote who settled Hartford, Connecticut (1637), Edward Cartwright who migrated to Nantucket Island, Massachusetts (1672), and Henry Adams who took up residence in Braintree, Massachusetts (1632). Growing up in Allegany County in the 1950s and 1960s, I regularly walked or drove past many one-room school houses. Some have been razed, a few converted to museums, churches, and libraries, but the majority were incorporated into houses, making them almost unrecognizable as the education centers they once were. My elementary school education was within the red brick walls of a building that served as Alma Township's only high school and, with an addition, later housed grades K-12 in Allentown, New York.

One-room schools have always fascinated me because they were centers of learning where all grades were taught simultaneously and they were locally funded by the parents and the community without federal financial aid and almost no state educational assistance. During my doctoral work in Education, I studied the History of Education and taught History of Education courses at the undergraduate level. In both studying and teaching the History of Education, I increasingly looked back to Allegany County for examples about school curricula, educational programs, teacher qualifications, and school architecture to include in my research projects and lectures. In 1998, I presented a research paper on one-room school architecture at an international conference at the University of

Louvain in Belgium using visual examples of Allegany County's one-room schools.

Schools, one-room or larger, provided not just an education but engendered social interaction among all age groups in each township of Allegany County. One-room schools were a product of an agricultural America, which believed that education enriched one religiously and promoted both economic opportunity and social mobility. One-room schools anchored communities. The consolidation of schools in Allegany County from 1869 to 1910, from 1910 to 1945, and 1945 to 1998 forced the closure of one-room rural schools. As a consequence, hamlets declined and collapsed. Families relocated to incorporated villages where larger elementary schools were built and academies and/or high schools were established. School consolidation paralleled the shift of the United States from an agriculture based- to an industrial-based economy.

By the beginning of the 20th century American families took increasing pride in children educated to the sixth grade. Later, it was to the eighth grade, and by World War II, there was a greater desire by families to have their sons and daughters earn high school diplomas. The United States with its commitment to education, was a strong magnet attracting immigrants from Europe and Asia because education there was both expensive, limited, and families were restricted to the same occupations, generation after generation, without reprieve or opportunity. Some immigrants, particularly from central and southern Europe, made their way to Allegany County.

Over time I increasingly compared my educational experiences from kindergarten to the sixth grade in Allentown, New York and grades seven to twelve in Wellsville, New York with state, regional, and national norms in curricula, instruction quality, and teacher qualifications. In all aspects my educational experiences not only rivalled but exceeded the national norms. I was taught by a number of unmarried female teachers. Teaching was one of the few occupations open to women. I felt very lucky to have had many well qualified women, both single and married, who were so dedicated to the profession that they never restricted their time with students to a seven- or eight-hour work day. All of the women and men who were part of my educational experience from kindergarten to graduation were consistent in encouraging me to excel and succeed. For me, educational opportunity led to social mobility into career possibilities my parents or grandparents would never have considered for themselves.

In writing this history on one-room schools in Allegany County, I hope to return to the County and its residents a concise narrative in both words and pictures its educational history as a way to thank the educators and schools who nurtured me through thirteen years of learning. This project has been facilitated by the assistance of the Library of Congress' Map Division, which has allowed me to include the maps in this book. I extend a deep debt of gratitude to Mike C. Beaty for scanning in and cleaning up the many old photographs of one-room schools, high schools, and consolidated central schools. I want to thank David Dean, a fellow traveler with me through elementary and secondary school, for allowing the use of his watercolor *Fields of Learning* to grace the cover of this book and to use his title as part of my book title. David is an amazing self-taught artist in residence in Allegany County, New York. The visual record of Allegany County schools was accomplished by the generosity and assistance of Ron Taylor, President and Executive Director of the Allegany County Historical Society and Museum in Andover, New York. I accord special recognition to Jean Milliman, Genesee Township Historian, who led the campaign to save the Ceres, New York school, convert it into an historical museum, and obtain recognition of the school on the National Register of Historic Places. A final thank you to my teachers, all now deceased, at Allentown Union School who guided my initial journey into the realm of the educated: Miss Anna Storms (kindergarten), Mrs. Iona Swarthout (grades 1 and 2), Mrs. Estelle Aiken (grade 3), Mrs. Marjorie Richmond (grade 4), and Miss Helen Milliman (grades 5 and 6).

William A. Paquette, Ph.D.

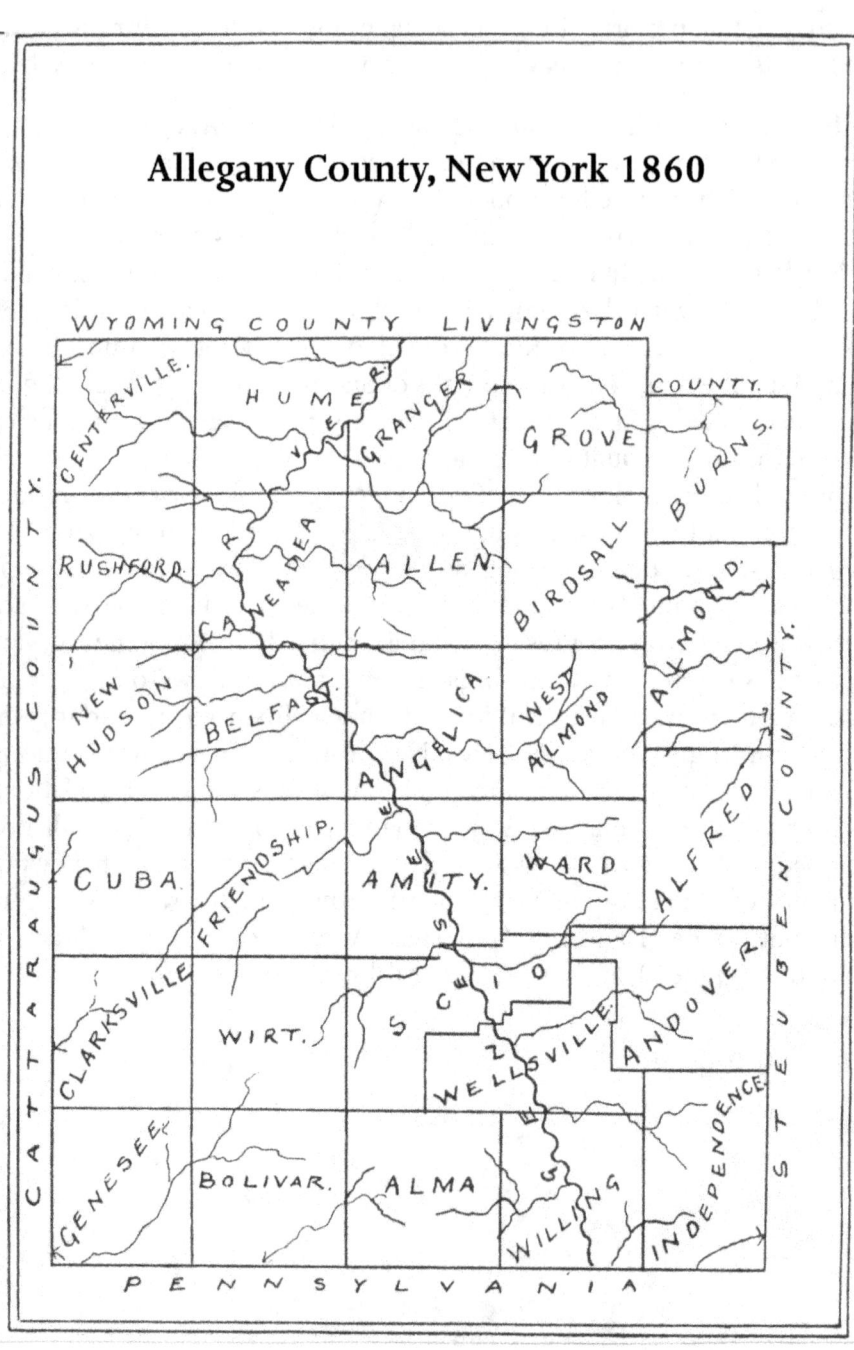

The 29 Townships of Allegany County, New York - 1860

CHAPTER ONE
One-Room Schools: A History, 1869 - 1945

The one-room schoolhouse in the history of United States education is institutionalized as the repository of the American values of independence, self-reliance, democracy, and simple rural virtues. The popular American television shows, *Little House on the Prairie* and the *Waltons,* most recently presented the one-room school as an idyllic learning environment, which gave every attendee equal opportunity to excel and achieve workplace social mobility as part of the local community. The reality of one-room schools across the United States was much closer to an educational system that personified inefficiency, incompetence, poor sanitation, malnourished students, and cultural provincialism. One-room schools were usually located on useless land, on hills or in hollows, close to population concentrations, or on small plots hemmed in by roads, tilled fields, swamps, and farmyards.[1] Nevertheless, the purpose of one-room schools was to educate and extend the virtues and democratic values of the United States to each new generation. As the photographs in this book and the accompanying statistics exemplify, Allegany County one-room schools were probably much better than the national norm.

Allegany County in southwestern New York State was created in the early 1800s from the Holland, Gorham, and Phelps land purchases of the Seneca Indians hunting grounds. The majority of the county's pioneer families were English of the Pilgrim or Puritan religious persuasion who walked west out of New England into New York State in search of farmland. In the 1820s, Allegany County was a land of primeval forest of full-grown oak, maple, hemlock, elm, and ash that formed canopied valleys. The trees were so far apart that a horse could be ridden through at a full gallop. The first homes were log houses. When the settlers were hungry all they had to do was to take an old flintlock rifle and go into the forest to bring down a deer. The streams were alive with trout and small game was plentiful.[2]

Allegany County's commitment to education was evidenced with the arrival of New Englanders, who established schools soon after houses were built in Almond (1802), Angelica (1804-5), Amity (1810), Wellsville (1811), and Scio and Granger (1819). The 1879 *History of Allegany County, New York* recorded that all the townships had schools by 1825. The educators for these early schools were usually men who were paid by the parents of the students they taught in either money or food and services. Private academies existed in Friendship (1848), Richburg (1848), Belfast (1848), and Rushford (1851) where the educators were usually men. By 1867, the private academies were changed to public Union Schools with funds supplied by parents, the community, local industry, and state financial assistance. Allegany County received its first state education support in 1813 in the amount of $58.86. Teacher training classes were taught at Alfred University, Genesee Valley Seminary and Union School, Wilson's Angelica School (named for Angelica resident Colonel William Wilson), Belmont and Friendship Union Schools, and the Wellsville School. This book's educational focus will be from 1869-1945 because the most complete record of education for Allegany County, New York's one-room schools exists for that time period.[3] It is clear that Allegany County was committed to education from its founding and its residents were willing to find and spend the money to make it happen.

Architecture

Andrew Gulliford wrote in *America's Country Schools* that schoolhouse architecture in the United States could be divided into four distinct periods and styles: *vernacular*, a primitive dwelling, like a log house, serving as a schoolhouse; *folk vernacular*, a simple dwelling with some ornamentation reflecting the traditions of the local population; *mass vernacular*, a structure resembling a schoolhouse but with features typical of a church or town hall; and *architect designed*, executed by a hired architect or copied from published design books. Frank W. Cyr and Henry H. Linn, authors of *Planning Rural Community School Buildings*, added a fifth architectural style, *monumental,* a multi-storied structure. Authors Gulliford, Cyr, and Linn located one-room schools along Main Street between churches and businesses, just outside of town, or along country crossroads.[4]

The topography of Allegany County's 29 townships is mostly hilly upland separated by the deep valleys of its streams with summits 500 to 800 feet above the valleys and 2,000 to 2,500 feet above tide. New England homesteaders were not deterred by the county's hills, which were too steep for profitable cultivation. Nor were they deterred by the Genesee River, which divided the county into two parts as it flows northward emptying into Lake Ontario. The 1865 Federal Census listed Allegany County's economy as agrarian based on the cultivation of wheat and spring grains and a dairy industry producing milk and cheese. Construction of the Genesee River Canal and the Erie Railroad guaranteed future economic growth.[5]

The population of Allegany County's 29 townships was dispersed by its agrarian based economy.[6] In 1869, the number of residents for the county's 65 villages each numbered from 50 to 200 people. Nineteenth-century histories on Allegany County described the first schools as resembling log houses, *vernacular style*; situated along dirt roads connecting the county's small villages. School attendance must have been very irregular given the distances needed to walk.[7]

Henry Barnard in his 1838 plan book *School Architecture: Or, Contributions to the Improvement of School-Houses in the United States*, suggested that schoolhouse sites should overlook delightful country and present both sunshine and shade, flowers and trees, and be sheltered from prevailing winds.[8] More accurate, perhaps, was John R. Stilgoe's commentary on school house sites in *Common Landscape of America, 1580-1910*, which indicated that site selection frequently caused trouble between neighbors. A farmer or village resident who donated the land for a schoolhouse could demand the property back. Many farmers did not want the school near their property because children could damage the crops when taking short cuts. Therefore, any sliver of land not fit for agriculture near swamps, mud holes, floodplains, or even near pigsties could become a location for a school.[9] Records for Allegany County indicate that prominent farmers or merchants donated land for schools. Rural schools in Allegany County were usually built on less productive farmland and in town near the business property of the person who donated the land.

The 1869 Beers Insurance Maps located 90% of Allegany County's village schools on Main Street or just outside of the business district but still on the main road into town with rural schools constructed where several farm properties and roads intersected. Ten percent of the county's villages built their schools in residential neighborhoods near a church or a cemetery.[10] In 1869, Allegany County had 310 one-room schools among its 29 townships.[11] That averages to almost eleven one-room schools per township. I suggest that the high number was directly linked to the residents New England religious and cultural heritage, which placed great emphasis on literacy in order to read the Bible.

Photographs and statistical data on Allegany County's one-room schools survive for 17 of the county's 29 townships.[12] The majority of the seventeen townships were located in the southern half of the county where oil was discovered in 1881, transforming the region from an agrarian society to an industrial-based economy. As the population increased the log schools, *vernacular style,* were replaced by larger one-room schools constructed in the *folk vernacular* style. The only surviving photographic record, which resembles *vernacular* style, was Allentown, New York's original school with wood siding instead of logs.

Allentown NY— Vernacular Style

This building in the 20th century was a popular restaurant known as *Mildred's Diner* and today is a private residence. One hundred of the remaining 119 one-room schools for which a photographic record exists were in the *folk vernacular* architectural style. The county's *folk vernacular* schoolhouses resembled agricultural outbuildings, rarely had ornamental detailing, and were seldom painted. They displayed the American flag, were built in an area devoid of trees, frequently on hillsides, with an outhouse nearby. Most folk vernacular schools had a single entrance with two or three windows on two sides of the building. The range of the human voice and vision shaped the school's length.[13] An excellent example of *folk vernacular* architecture in Allegany County was the District 6 School, outside Bolivar, New York, in Kossuth, which survives and today is used as a church.

Bolivar District 6 School, Kossuth, NY—Folk Vernacular Style

Nineteen school houses were examples of the *mass vernacular* style of design, which Gulliford described as using commercial machine-made materials producing a structure that looked more like a schoolhouse than a farm building. Ornamental details included porticos, dormers, bell towers, columns, and even gingerbread.[14] Eighteen of the nineteen *mass vernacular* schools in Allegany County resembled town halls and churches more than a schoolhouse. The District 8 Friendship School provides a very expressive example of *mass vernacular architecture* resembling a church more than a school. *(See Next Page)*

Friendship District 8—Mass Vernacular Style

The Alfred District 1 School, Alfred Station, New York might be an example of an *architect designed* school with its cupola supported by a brick structure with a columned entrance and terra cotta roof tiles. The author does not know if this structure was designed by an architect, but the building conveys the impression that, maybe, it was.

Alfred District 1 School, Alfred Station, NY—Architect Designed Style

Monumental, multi-storied architecture in Allegany County schools were unlikely to be one-room but would have included all elementary grades as well as grades seven and eight. The Spring Mills Academy in southern Independence Township, Allegany County, New York would be a perfect visual example of this form of educational architecture.

Spring Mills Academy, Independence Township—Monumental Style

Economic prosperity from the discovery of oil provided the necessary revenue for Allegany County school districts at the end of the 19th century to build two- and three-story wood, brick, and stone structures for secondary schools. No new elementary schools were built. Existing one-room schools remained structurally unchanged and some were in use until 1945. Elementary and Secondary grades were housed in separate buildings. High schools were designed by architects hired by a school district and/or copied from a plan book. The Romanesque style was used exclusively for Allegany County high schools in Greek revival, Queen

Anne, Classical Revival, Mission, Bungalow, or International architect design style.[15] The Romanesque high schools were usually topped by a bell tower and located on residential streets away from business and commerce. Richburg High School or Academy in Richburg, New York exemplifies the popularity of Romanesque architecture sweeping the United States in the last decades of the 19th century.

The interior of the typical one-room school had tongue-and-groove flooring, wainscoting, embossed metal ceilings, cast iron desks, cabinets, shelving, and slate blackboards. Desks needed to accommodate anyone from age five to 20 years. The typical desk consisted of a stationary seat back and desk top with a wooden seat that folded. The back of the desk was the writing surface for the person seated behind. Each desk contained an inkwell. Desks were arranged in three rows facing the teacher's desk. A potbellied stove centered the room. Boys sat on the east row and girls in the west row. The middle row contained the overflow from the other two rows. The room's total space was to be 28 by 40 feet with a height of 15 feet. Wardrobes on the side reduced the classroom space to 28 by 32 feet. The space could seat up to fifty students, but seldom did. The teacher's desk was on a platform in the front of the room. Blackboards were recommended to be five feet wide and wrapped around the entire room. Wainscoting rose 4 ½ feet from the floor to the just below the windows. A typical building had three windows on each side of the building paralleling the rows of seats.[16]

Enrollments/Expenditures

By 1910, Allegany County's population was significantly shifting from farming to village centered oil production and manufacturing in both the central and southern part of the county. The number of one-room schools in the county decreased to 219. The surviving data on seventeen of the county's twenty-nine townships, the central and southern parts, reveal the amount of state aid provided, student enrollments, average student attendance, assessed valuation for school properties, school expenses, teacher education levels, and the educational cost per pupil.[17] Tables 1, 2, and 3 summarize this data.

Enrollments for 1910 among Allegany County's seventeen townships one-room elementary schools averaged 35 students with a range from a low of 11 students for Belfast Township to 51 students for Andover

TABLE # 1

ELEMENTARY/SECONDARY SCHOOLS

ALLEGANY COUNTY, NEW YORK TOWNSHIPS, 1910**

School Feature~	Alma (7/8) *	Bolivar (7/8) *	Clarksville (7/7) *	Genesee (5/5) *	Scio (8/8) *	Wirt (11/11) *
State aid	$ 205.00	$ 136.00	$ 164.00	$ 174.00	$ 216.58	$ 190.90
Enrollment	27 students	21 students	21 students	35 students	28 students	22 students
Ave. Attendance	19 students	15 students	15 students	24 students	21 students	16 students
Assessed Valuation	$ 70,217.28	$ 86,783.29	$ 48,039.86	$ 90,770.60	$ 89,178.50	$ 64,611.00
Expenditures	$ 1,233.53	$ 490.80	$ 562.42	$ 769.03	$ 1,078.25	$ 776.89
cost/capita	$ 38.00	$ 29.90	$ 30.96	$ 23.25	$ 34.10	$ 37.38
tax rate	.017	.00430	.00735	.006094	.0069375	.00619

~ Figures are averages based on the number of schools reporting.

* Indicates the number of schools reporting within each township.

** Statistics compiled from Thomas E. Finegan's *Elementary Education Report for the School Year Ending July 31, 1916*.

TABLE # 2

ELEMENTARY/SECONDARY SCHOOLS

ALLEGANY COUNTY, NEW YORK TOWNSHIPS, 1910**

School Feature~	Alfred (7/7) *	Andover (8/9) *	Independence (5/6) *	Ward (7/7) *	Wellsville (7/8) *	Willing (6/6) *
State aid	$ 459.64	$ 311.32	$ 155.00	$ 180.71	$ 166.43	$ 156.67
Enrollment	48 students	51 students	18 students	14 students	21 students	24 students
Ave. Attendance	37 students	38 students	13 students	10 students	15 students	17 students
Assessed Valuation	$ 91,656.57	$ 90,572.13	$ 88,005.60	$ 33,313.71	$ 73,879.57	$ 54,565.83
Expenditures	$ 1,924.48	$ 1,421.60	$ 1,037.19	$ 400.73	$ 516.24	$ 497.57
cost/capita	$ 27.49	$ 28.49	$ 28.34	$ 31.68	$ 30.70	$ 22.85
tax rate	.00826	.00723	.00414	.0088414	.00523	.01323

~ Figures are averages based on the number of schools reporting.

* Indicates the number of schools reporting within each township.

** Statistics compiled from Thomas E. Finegan's *Elementary Education Report for the School Year Ending July 31, 1916*.

Township. However, actual attendance averaged 18 students with a low of 8, again for Belfast Township, and a high of 38 for Andover Township. The average cost per capita in 1910 was $30.58 per student. The lowest cost per student was $13.47 in Cuba Township and a high of $53.56 per student for Belfast Township, which had the lowest enrollments. New York State aid to Allegany County's seventeen townships averaged $224.99 per township with Bolivar Township receiving the lowest amount per student at $136.00 while Alfred Township was given state aid of $459.64 per student. The assessed valuation of school property for the seventeen townships averaged at $65,845.20. Cuba Township had the highest valuation at $99,120.60 while Belfast Township had the lowest at $39,367.00. Expenditures for the seventeen townships averaged $708.32 with Belfast Township spending the least at $376.65 and Alfred Township the most at $1,934.48.[18]

TABLE # 3

ELEMENTARY/SECONDARY SCHOOLS

ALLEGANY COUNTY, NEW YORK TOWNSHIPS, 1910**

School Feature+	Amity (7/8) *	Belfast (6/7) *	Cuba (5/7) *	Friendship (5/8) *	New Hudson (11/12) *
State Aid	$ 169.86	$ 153.37	$ 150.00	$ 175.00	$ 160.02
Enrollment	27 students	11 students	28 students	15 students	18 students
Ave. Attendance	17 students	8 students	14 students	10 students	11 students
Assessed Valuation	$ 86,378.00	$ 39,367.00	$ 99,120.60	$ 44,486.40	$ 51,626.55
Expenditures	$ 552.38	$ 376.65	$ 487.54	$ 403.55	$ 452.68
Cost/capita	$ 23.81	$ 53.56	$ 13.47	$ 34.32	$ 31.54
tax rate	.00748	.0041733	.00425	.005796	.0056981

+   Figures are averages based on the number of schools reporting.

*   Indicates the number of schools reporting within each township.

**   Statistics compiled from Thomas E. Finegan's *Elementary Education Report for the School Year Ending July 31, 1916.*

What does the data mean? The northern portion of Allegany County was still primarily a farming region in 1910. It was also the poorer section of Allegany County, not benefiting from the oil boom in the southern half and manufacturing along the Erie Railroad in the central portion. Therefore, Belfast Township reflected an economic disparity within Allegany County. Oil production existed for Cuba Township and this offered more monies for education. This was also true for Andover Township. Alfred Township educationally benefited from Alfred University[19] location within the township and the emphasis placed on higher education naturally spilled over into lower educational levels. Surprisingly, some of the richest townships, e.g. Bolivar, Genesee, Wirt, and Wellsville received lower amounts of state aid. However, state aid was not designed to fully fund township education, but to compensate for a lack of funding from other township sources including property taxes and oil revenue. Some of these schools benefited directly from oil wealth and were organized as *Union* schools, separating them from public schools.

Union schools were financed entirely by the residents who sent their children to the school and oil revenue set aside by the township. Allentown Union School in Alma Township, where I attended elementary school, was the recipient of state aid, property taxes allocated for schools, and a percentage of oil revenue profits. In 1959, the decline in oil production forced Allentown Union School to merge with a public school in neighboring Scio Township to offer a broader range of course offerings and to cover the increasing cost of education. The enrollment figures in Charts 1, 3, and 5, are only for the seventeen townships' one-room schools in the rural areas and do not include the high school enrollments or township elementary schools that either shared a multi-storied building with a high school or had their own two- to three-story structures. Therefore, it is not possible to calculate the total educational enrollments for Allegany County's schools in 1910.

In 1910, seventeen of the County's twenty-nine townships had functioning high schools.

Teacher Education

Teacher education for the seventeen townships' one-room schools included teachers whose credentials came from the following training options: college graduate, college graduate limited, normal school, professional development, temporary license, training class, training class sub-academic, first-grade certificate, rural school renewable, permanent equivalency, and academic certificate. Tables 4, 5, and 6 summarize this data for seventeen of the County's twenty-nine townships. In 1910 there were 145 teachers dispersed among the one-room schools for seventeen of Allegany County's townships. Ninety-nine of the 145 teachers earned teaching credentials from training classes. Teacher *training* classes were mandated by New York State and were taught in high schools.

TABLE # 4

TEACHER QUALIFICATIONS

ALLEGANY COUNTY, NEW YORK TOWNSHIPS, 1910**

TRAINING	Alma*	Bolivar	Clarksville	Genesee	Scio*	Wirt*
College Graduate						
College Grad. Ltd.	1				1	
Normal School	2			1	3	1
Professional Development						
Temporary License					1	
Training Class	6	6	7	4	5	9
Training Class Certificate Sub academic					1	1
1st Grade Certificate		1				
Rural School Renewable				1		2
Permanent Equivalency						1
Academic Certificate		1			1	1

*   Includes township high school.
** Statistics compiled from Thomas E. Finegan's *Elementary Education Report for the School Year Ending July 31, 1916.*

Prior to 1917, an applicant had to complete three years of high school. In 1917, the law was changed requiring four years of high school to be considered for teacher training. The training lasted for one year and centered on the fundamentals of the subjects taught in the elementary grades with the content applied to rural life problems. It was hoped that several years of teaching would encourage teachers from the training course to apply for admission to a normal school (for teacher education) with a more vigorous academic curriculum over four years of study. Fifteen educators were trained at normal schools or teacher colleges, three were college graduates, and three had some college education.

The remaining teachers were selected as educators based on obtaining a temporary license (six teachers), a training certificate sub-academic (4 teachers), first grade certificate (four teachers), rural school renewal

TABLE # 5

TEACHER QUALIFICATIONS

ALLEGANY COUNTY, NEW YORK TOWNSHIPS, 1910**

Training	Alfred*	Andover*	Independence	Ward	Wellsville	Willing
College Graduate	1	2				
College Graduate Ltd.	1					
Normal School	3	3				
Professional Development	2					
Temporary License		2				
Training Class	7	5	5	6	6	6
Training Class Certificate Sub academic				1		
1st Grade Certificate		1			1	
Rural School Renewable						
Permanent Equivalency						
Academic Certificate	1					

*   Includes township high school.

** Statistics compiled from Thomas E. Finegan's *Elementary Education Report for the School Year Ending July 31, 1916*.

certificate (3 teachers), permanent equivalency (one teacher), and five teachers held academic certificates. The townships with teachers who were either college graduates or teachers with some college education taught in Alma, Alfred, Andover, and Scio townships. It is unclear if these townships offered higher salaries or if the teachers had family ties in these communities. What is clear is that Allegany County's one-room school teachers were professionally trained with 83% of the teaching staff holding a Training Certificate or a college degree.[20] Elementary school teachers were usually women and frequently single. Married women who were teachers usually entered the profession after their children were grown or in widowhood. Administrators were always male.

TABLE # 6

TEACHER QUALIFICATIONS

ALLEGANY COUNTY, NEW YORK TOWNSHIPS, 1910**

Training	Amity	Belfast	Cuba	Friendship	New Hudson
College Graduate					
College Graduate Ltd.					
Normal School	1	1			
Professional Development					
Temporary License					3
Training Class	5	4	5	5	8
Training Class Sub academic	1				
1st Grade Certificate		1			
Rural School Renewable					
Permanent Equivalency					
Academic Certificate	1				

** Statistics compiled from Thomas E. Finegan's *Elementary Education Report for the School Year Ending July 31, 1916.*

Teacher Responsibilities

Teachers were required to attend their respective departments at least twenty minutes before the opening of school in the morning and afternoon. Teachers were responsible for the good behavior of the pupils in the classroom and in the building. Promotions or holding back a student had to have the approval of the Principal. No student could be suspended without the Principal's approval. Teachers were required to be attentive to their student's physical education and comfort to promote their moral development including the regulation of temperature and ventilation. Educators were required to attend semi-monthly teachers' meetings and work with the principal to develop harmony in the work place. Teachers were required to maintain records on each student. Teacher grievances were to be communicated to the Principal and could be made to the school board in writing.

The success of a teacher can be measured by the success of each student. Teachers were to be acquainted with the parents and guardians of their pupils in order to better understand their students' behaviors, temperaments, and needs. Teachers were expected to teach word along with their meanings. Pupils were not to be pushed beyond what they could reasonably achieve in a school day. It was the obligation of teachers to correct common errors of speech as quickly as possible and to place before students only correct forms of speech. Work that was mechanical without thought was to be avoided. Student work was to be neat and well done. Students were to talk intelligently and pronounce all words correctly. The chief aim of a teacher was to develop the natural order of the child's mind. Make work as inductive as possible. Always have children read together with the teacher. The primary goal of education was the cultivation of intellect, not the acquisition of knowledge. Teachers were to be patient with dull pupils to help them distinguish between failure and inability. Each student was to be surrounded by the environment necessary to achieve good classroom results. Teachers were responsible, to an extent, for the moral, physical, and intellectual training of each pupil. Education should not consist of listening and imitation but in active, original endeavor, active, original work achieved by the student's own faculties.[21]

The Pupils

New York State in 1894 enacted into law a requirement that children between the ages of seven and fourteen were required to attend school between October and June annually. Children between fourteen and sixteen were required to attend school for only eighty days a year given their labor was needed to supplement the family income by working on the family farm, in factories, mills, mines, or sweat shops. In 1903 the New York State legislature amended the 1894 law to require boys between fourteen and sixteen who had not completed an elementary education to attend evening school. In 1913 the education law was again changed requiring boys to have six years of completed elementary education before seeking employment. The school year for boys ages fourteen to sixteen was extended to 180 days, the full school year. In 1916 education was made compulsory to fifteen years for both boys and girls. Failure of students to attend schools could result in a fine of $5 for the first offense and for each subsequent offense to a maximum of $50 or imprisonment of

Fields of Learning

the parent for 30 days. Any individual employing a student between the ages of fourteen and sixteen years, were subject to fines of between $20 and $50. However, a student between the ages of fourteen and sixteen, deemed necessary to the family's welfare, could work if proper approved forms were completed.[22]

Strict rules were applied to enrolled students. Pupils were to render prompt and cheerful obedience to teacher demands and be courteous to each other. Students were to complete required work promptly and thoroughly. If a pupil displayed negligent and careless behavior, the teacher would contact the parent or guardian and the student in question could be demoted to a lower class. Violent or incorrigible behavior was reported to the principal (a man) who contacted the School Board for action. The destruction of school property had to be repaired or paid for within three days, and if not, the student could be suspended.

Absences of more than ten days from classroom attendance could lead to suspension. Students were not permitted to leave school before the regular hour for closing without written permission of the parent or guardian unless they were taken ill. The return to school after an absence had to be accompanied by a written explanation from the parent. Students were not permitted to use profane or obscene language on school property. They were not allowed to bring firearms, weapons, or explosives. The use of tobacco was prohibited. Throwing and batting of stones was banned as was the entering of classroom without the permission of a teacher. Enrolled pupils were required to provide their own school books, stationery and other materials needed for classroom use. Students were not allowed to miss examinations and if enrolled in advanced classes parents were requested to allow students extra time at home from their chores to complete their work.

Promotion was determined by an evaluation of proficiency based on a series of four written reviews and a final examination at the end of the term. A student must attain an average of 75 percent and not fall below a 65 percent average in any study area. Teacher recommendation with the approval of the principal could permit a student promotion if it was determined that holding the student back would not benefit the student.

Grade promotions were made each September.[23]

Curricula

Grade One: One-room schools did not have kindergarten. Therefore, first grade was the start of the educational journey for students. The first semester of grade one taught reading, spelling, language, numbers, places (right, left, and the position of objects), and lessons on cleanliness and manners. The second half of the first year continued reading with a reader, language, numbers, color (standard colors), the human body (naming of body parts), writing, and drawing. Parents were encouraged to have their children read the following books: picture books with animals, *Jack and Jill*, books of nursery rhymes, *Grimus* (sic) *Fairy Tales*, *Mother Goose*, and *Stories of Heroic Deeds*. Other selections included: *Child's Garden of Verses* by Stevenson, *Nine World* (Norse Stories) by Litchfield, *All Things Bright and Beautiful* by Alexander, and *Years at the Spring* by Browning.

Grade Two: Promotion to grade two started with reading and the formation of sentences. Students were taught numbers to 20, times tables, and Roman numerals. Penmanship, drawing, and general and observation lessons completed the curricula for the first semester. The second semester continued progress in the reader to page 40, number counting from 40 to 100 along with times tables by fours, fives, and sixes, and Roman numerals. Penmanship, drawing, and general and observation lessons were continued. Recommended outside reading included: *Stories of the Red Children* by Brooks, *Rhymes and Jingles* by Dodge, *Books of Fables* by Scudder, *Stories of Great Americans* by Eggleston, and *Anderson's Fairy Tales* by Turpin.

Grade Three: Grade 3, first term, introduced the concept of minus in arithmetic, ordinals to 150, times tables by sevens, eights, nines, and tens, Roman numerals and problem-solving using multiplication tables. Drawing and form study were continued along with penmanship with sentences. The second semester's goal was to complete the second reader and begin supplementary reading. Times tables by elevens and twelves were taught along with numbers to 1000, Roman numerals, subtraction, and a review of the first and second grade work for promotion consideration to Grade 4. Outside reading included the following choices: *Big People and Little People of other Lands* by Shaw, *Sandman* (Farm Life Stories) by Hopkins, *Ring of the Golden River* by Ruskin, and *Buz-Buz* (Story of the Bee) by Pratt. Additional options included *Old Greek Stories* by Baldwin, *Historical and Bibliographical Narratives* by Wallach, *Pasy Ring* by Wiggin's and Smith, and *Poems that Every Child Should Know* by Burt.

Grade Four: The fourth year of elementary education reviewed the second reader and added supplementary reading selections twice a week. Addition to 900 was covered and practice with subtraction. Spelling was based on words from the second reader. Copy books were required for writing practice three times a week. Drawing was taught twice a week. Oral and written language instruction included basic concepts on grammar. Poetry was introduced by the end of the first semester. The second semester of grade 4 introduced the third reader with supplementary reading including poetry. Continued practice with addition and subtraction was undertaken with spelling words coming from the third reader. Language grammar with practice in phonics and stories with pictures were presented. Geography lessons involving town, county, and state was started. Simple designs were the objectives for drawing. By fourth grade students were encouraged to read *Alice's Adventures in Wonderland* by Carroll, *Story of a Bad Boy* by Aldrich, Kipling's *Jungle Book*, *Children of the Cold* (manners and customs for child) by Schwatker, and *Boys of Other Countries* by Taylor. Additional selections included: *Arabian Nights* by Clarke, *Tales of King Arthur* by Farrington, *Story of Siegfried* and *Horse Fair* by Baldwin, and *Wonder Clock* (stories of other lands) by Pyle.

Grade Five: Grade 5, first semester, continued with the third reader and vocabulary. Addition and subtraction were reviewed along with multiplication using mental testing. Roman numerals from 500 to 1000 were explained and notations to 100,000 in regular arithmetic. Spelling words were based on the reader. Geography was studied for the United States and the World. Special topics in geography focused on New York State and New England. Students practiced map drawing. Basic lessons in civics and history were introduced. Students began to write compositions. Studies were undertaken about plants and animals. The second semester focus was all four processes in arithmetic: addition, subtraction, multiplication, and division. The fourth reader was begun and word building introduced. Spelling words were reader based. *Barnes Elementary Geography* and *Writing Book No. 5* were introduced. Students continued composition writing and taking dictation. Drawing lessons involved form study and working drawings were made. Students were encouraged to read on their own the following selections: *The Boy's Iliad* and *The Boy's Odyssey* by Perry, Hawthorne's *Wonder Book* and *Tanglewood Tales*, Pyle's *King Arthur and His Knights*, Gueber's *Legends of the Middle Ages*, Matthews *Poems of American Patriotism*, and *Poems that Every Child Should Know* by Burt.

Grade Six: The final grade for many students was grade 6. Students continued to use the fourth reader with spelling practice based on reader words. More attention was given to penmanship in work submitted. Geography lessons included the study of South America with government and history lessons based on *Eggleston's Beginners U.S. History*. Composition involved story writing and short composition work about plants and the human skeleton. Lessons about the negative effects of alcohol and narcotics were introduced. Drawing's focus was solids of varying types. The last semester of grade 6 centered on a review of arithmetic using Milne's Pro. Series, Second Book. The fourth reader and supplementary readings with spelling words coming from readings were grade 6 goals. Students continued their study of geography, civics, and U.S. history. Further discussions on the negative results of alcohol and narcotics use continued. In drawing students studied pattern-making and paper cutting. Recommended outside reading for Grade 6 was: *Little Women* and *Little Men* by Alcott, *Jack Hall, Stories for Boys* by Grant, *Betty Leister, Story for Girls* by Jewett, *Light Princess and Fairy Story* by MacDonald, *Knights of the Round Table* by Frost, *Ten Great Events in History* by Johonnot, Baldwin's *Story of Roland*, and Pyle's *Some Merry Adventures of Robin Hood*.[24]

The beginning of the 20th Century witnessed increased demand for students to continue their education beyond the sixth grade. Many one-room schools, as financial resources allowed and teacher staff was available, may have offered courses for grades 7 and 8. However, it was more likely that attending grades 7 and 8 would have been in one of Allegany County's hamlets or villages where the elementary or grammar schools had multiple classrooms in buildings with two floors.

Grade 7: Students during the first term of grade 7 studied the fifth reader in grade 7 and the use of the dictionary. Quotations were memorized. Students were expected to write original compositions for language and Milne's Book Three Project Series was used for arithmetic. In Geography students studied the North Central Sates. Map drawing was intensified. Eggleston's History Advanced Natural School Geography book was used. In Physiology Overton's Intermediate textbook was used. During the second term of seventh grade students studied geometric forms for drawing, continued to use the Fifth Reader with emphasis on poetry and prose, and learned the proper use of stems, prefixes, and suffixes in spelling. In grammar special attention was given to letter writing. The Arithmetic textbook continued to be Book Three and the History utilized Eggleston. In Geography Europe was studied with additional emphasis on the cities of this continent. In Physiology, the digestive organs were studied and students were warned about the adverse impact of alcohol and narcotic use. Time was spent at the seventh-grade level for student preparation for the state-wide Regents' exams.

Students were encouraged to undertake supplementary readings in *Tom Brown's School Days* by Hughes, *The Prince and the Pauper* by Twain, *Poolly Oliver's Problem and How One Girl Solved self-support* by Wiggins, and Coles' *Story of Sonny Sahib, Life in India*. Additional options included Mabie's *Norse Stories Retold from the Eddas*, Chapin's *Story of the Rheingold*, Hawthorne's *Grandfather's Chair*, Hale's *Man Without a Country*, and Wiggins and Smith poetry selections.

Grade 8: In the eighth grade more time was used by students and teachers to prepare for Regents' examinations in drawing, grammar, reading, arithmetic, geography, and physiology. Regents' examinations were (and continue to be) state-wide examinations with expectations that all students regardless of the school are able to meet certain standards of learning.

At the eighth-grade level students were expected to read at least three books for the following list: *Ulysses S. Grant, Hero Tales from American History, Talisman, Treasure Island, Sketch Book, Tales of a Traveler, Oregon*

Trail, Land of the Long Night, Two Years Before the Mast, Santa Claus' Partner, Standish of Standish, English Life in Colonies, As You Like it, Julius Caesar, Merchant of Venice, Iliad Tradition, Wake Robbin, My Summer in a Garden, Narrative Sketches from Tennyson, Browning, Bryon, Scott, Lowell, Hawthorne, Mabie, Van Dyke, and Burroughs.[25]

Endnotes

1   Brown, Ray B. and Marshall Fishwick, *Icons in America* (Bowling Green: Bowling Green State University Press, 1978, p. 139, 145, 156.

2   Paquette, William, *The Root Family of Bolivar, New York* (Baltimore: Gateway Press, 1991), p. 7.

3   Beers, F. W. *The History of Allegany County, New York* (New York: F.W. Beers & Co., 1879), pp. 163, 166-7, and 171.

4   Gulliford, Andrew, *America's Country Schools* (Washington, DC: The Preservation Press, 1984), p. 164-5 and Cyr, Frank W. and Henry H. Linn, *Planning Rural Community School Buildings* (New York: Teachers College Press, Columbia University, 1949), p. 54-5.

5   Minard, John S., *Allegany County and its People* (Alfred, NY: W. A. Fergusson and Co., 1896), p. 21-9.

6   The townships of Angelica, Birdsall, Centerville, Scio, Ward, West Almond, and Wellsville had only one village each. Alfred, Allen, Alma, Almond, Amity, Andover, Belfast, Clarksville, Friendship, Genesee, Granger, Grove, Independence, Rushford, and Wirt Townships each had two villages. Bolivar, Caneadea, Cuba, and New Hudson each had three villages. Hume and Burns Townships had four villages apiece while Willing Township had five villages.

7   This same story is repeated without elaboration in all of the centennial and sesquicentennial histories listed in the bibliography.

8   Gulliford, op. cit., p. 161.

9   Ibid, p. 162. The reference lists writings by Wayne E. fuller, John Brinckerhoff Jackson, Fred Schroeder, and Eric Sloane.

10   Schools built in residential neighborhoods were in the villages of Alfred, Belmont, Caneadea, Cuba, and Oramel.

11   This calculation is based on a review of all Beer's Insurance Maps for Allegany County in 1869.

12   The photographs included in this article are from the personal collection of Dr. William Paquette.

13   Gulliford, op. cit., p. 165.

14   Ibid, p. 167.

15   High schools were built in Bolivar, Richburg (Wirt), Allentown (Alma), Wellsville, Scio, Whitesville (Independence), Andover, Alfred, Almond, Belmont (Amity), Friendship, Cuba, and Belfast. Fred Schroeder confirms in *Little Red Schoolhouse* the popularly of the Romanesque style as a truly American look.

16   Gulliford, op. cit., pp. 188-191.

17   1910 data exists for the following Allegany County Townships: Alfred, Alma, Amity, Andover, Belfast, Bolivar, Clarksville, Cuba, Friendship, Genesee, Independence, New Hudson, Scio, Ward, Wellsville, Willing, Wirt

18   Finegan, Thomas E., *Elementary Education, Report for the School Year Ending July 31, 1916*, (Albany, New York: University of the State of New York, 1917), entire book.

19   Alfred University was founded in 1836.

20   Finegan, op. cit., p. 507.

21   University of the State of New York, *Allentown Union High School, 1909-1910*, (Albany, New York: University of the State of New York, 1910, pages not numbered.

22   University of the State of New York, *Course of Study and Syllabus for Elementary Schools*, (Albany, New York: University of the State of New York), 1910, p. 139-41.

23   University of the State of New York, *Allentown Union High School, 1909-1910*, (Albany, New York: University of the State of New York), 1910, pages not numbered.

24   Ibid, pages not numbered in the book for grades 1 thru 6.

25   Ibid, pages not number for grades 7 and 8.

Chapter Two
One-Room Schools: A Photographic Essay

In 1869, Allegany County, New York had 310 one-room schools distributed across twenty-nine townships. Unfortunately, photographic images of all of the County's schools do not exist. This chapter will share 119 photographs of one-room schools taken between 1900 and 1915 and in the possession of the Allegany County Historical Society and Museum. All but three photographs are from the townships in central and southern Allegany County. Currently there are no photographs for one-room schools when they were educational centers for the townships of Birdsall, West Almond, Allen, Caneadea, Centerville, Hume, Granger, and Grove. There is one photograph each for one school in the townships of Almond, Angelica, and Burns.

The vast majority of photographic images correspond to the data available for the seventeen of Allegany County's twenty-nine townships discussed in the previous chapter. These schools are organized into three groups corresponding to the available maps which locate the County's one-room schools. However, there are a few township schools missing from this photographic record for the seventeen townships. The missing schools are the elementary schools for hamlets and incorporated villages, which were more than one-room. Amity Township has four more one-room school images than map locations. There is no Genesee District 2 school to explain the gap between Genesee District 1 and Genesee District 3. Two elementary schools are located within Bolivar village. Ward District 8 School does not have an image. Wellsville village had three elementary schools within the village boundaries and there are two township schools not pictured. No picture could be found for Willing District 7. In all three groups the schools are identified by their official township district number. Many, if not all of them, had other names recognizing their sponsor or location, but are not referred to by these alternative names. The township school photograph with its district number can be used to locate the school on the township maps.

New Hudson, Belfast, Cuba, Friendship, Amity Townships

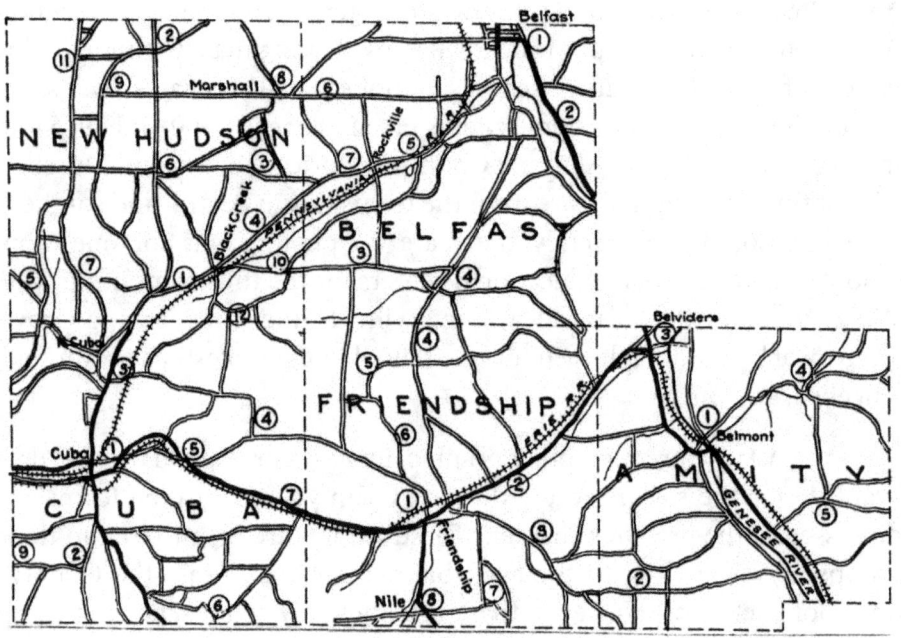

Allegheny County Township Map with School Districts Annotated

New Hudson School District

New Hudson District 1 School

New Hudson District 2 School

New Hudson District 3 School

New Hudson District 4 School

One-Room Schools: A Photographic Essay

New Hudson District 5 School

New Hudson District 6 School

New Hudson District 7 School

New Hudson District 8 School

New Hudson District 9 School

New Hudson District 10 School

New Hudson District 11 School

New Hudson District 11 School

Belfast School District

Belfast District 2 School

Belfast District 3 School

Belfast District 4 School

Belfast District 5 School

One-Room Schools: A Photographic Essay

Belfast District 6 School

Belfast District 7 School

Cuba School District

Cuba District 2 School

Cuba District 2 School

One-Room Schools: A Photographic Essay

Cuba District 4 School

Cuba District 6 School

Cuba District 7 School

Friendship School District

Friendship District 1 School

One-Room Schools: A Photographic Essay

Friendship District 3 School

Friendship District 4 School

Friendship District 5 School

Friendship District 6 School

Friendship District 7 School

Friendship District 8 School

Amity School District

Amity District 2 School

Amity District 3 School

Amity District 4 School

Amity District 5 School

Amity District 6 School

Amity District 7 School

One-Room Schools: A Photographic Essay

Amity District 8 School

Clarksville, Wirt, Scio, Genesee, Bolivar, Alma Townships

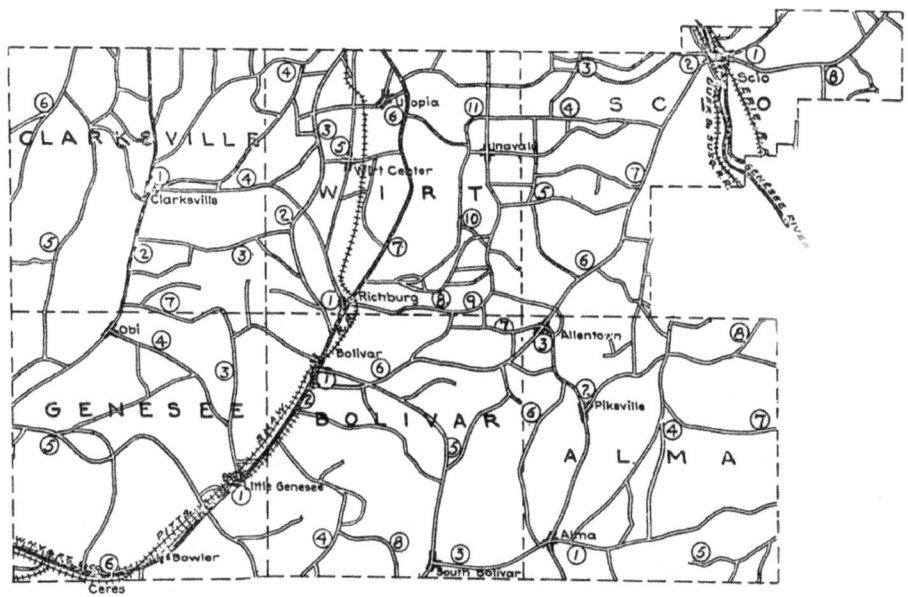
Allegheny County Township Map with School Districts Annotated

Clarksville School District

Clarksville District 1 School

Clarksville District 2 School

One-Room Schools: A Photographic Essay

Clarksville District 3 School

Clarksville District 4 School

Clarksville District 5 School

Clarksville District 6 School

Clarksville District 7 School

Wirt School District

Wirt District 2 School

Wirt District 3 School

Wirt District 4 School

Wirt District 5 School

Wirt District 6 School

Wirt District 7 School

Wirt District 8 School

One-Room Schools: A Photographic Essay

Wirt District 9 School

Wirt District 10 School

Wirt District 11 School

Scio School District

Scio District 2 School

Scio District 3 School

Scio District 4 School

Scio District 5 School

Scio District 6 School

One-Room Schools: A Photographic Essay

Scio District 7 School

Scio District 8 School

Fields of Learning

Genesee School District

Genesee District 1 School

Genesee District 3 School

Genesee District 4 School

Genesee District 5 School

Fields of Learning

Genesee District 6 School

Bolivar School District

Bolivar District 3 School

One-Room Schools: A Photographic Essay

Bolivar District 4 School

Bolivar District 5 School

Bolivar District 6 School

Bolivar District 7 School

One-Room Schools: A Photographic Essay

Bolivar District 8 School

Alma School District

Alma District 1 School

Alma District 2 School

Alma District 3 School

One-Room Schools: A Photographic Essay

Alma District 4 School

Alma District 5 School

Alma District 6 School

Alma District 7 School

One-Room Schools: A Photographic Essay

Alma District 8 School

Ward, Alfred, Wellsville, Andover, Willing, Independence Townships

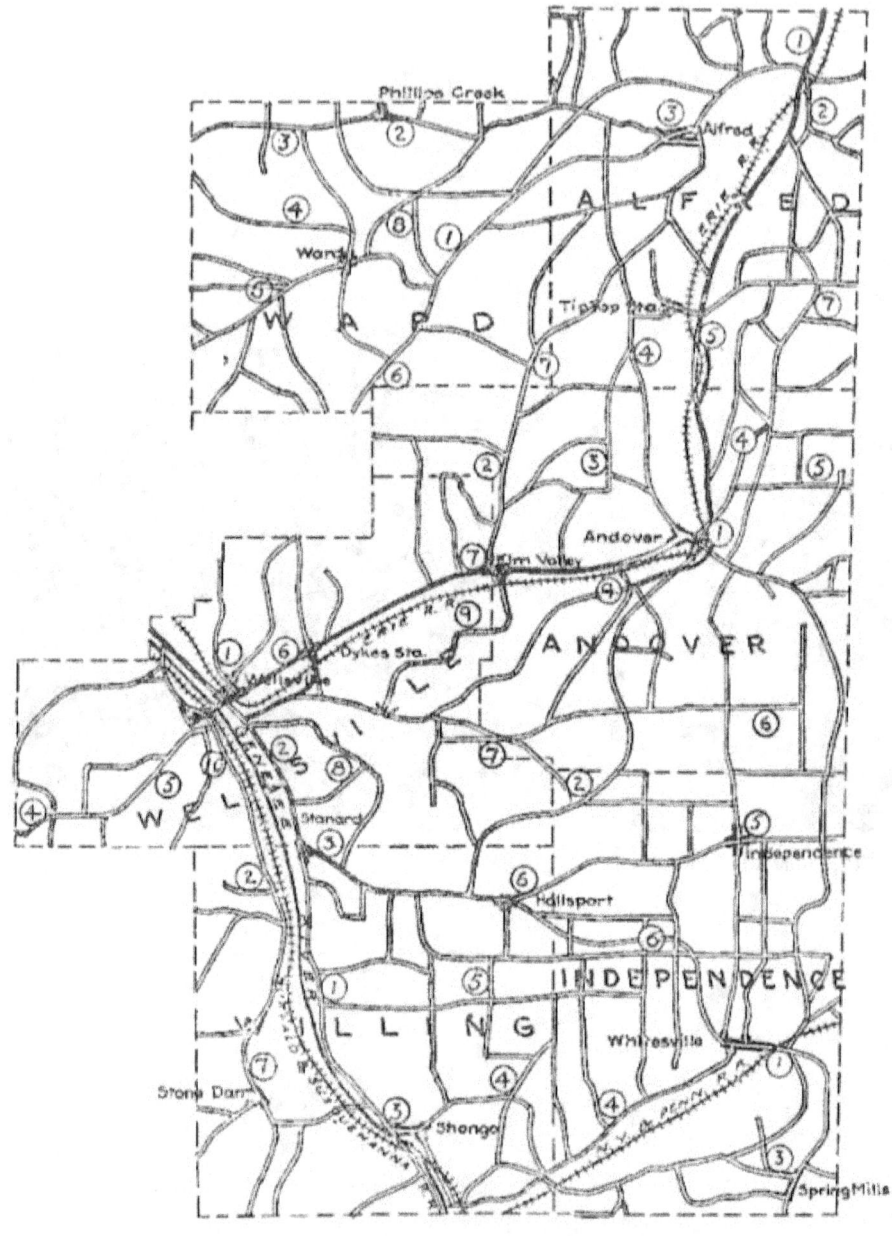

Allegheny County Township Map with School Districts Annotated

Ward School District

Ward District 1 School

Ward District 2 School

Ward District 3 School

Ward District 4 School

One-Room Schools: A Photographic Essay

Ward District 5 School

Ward District 6 School

Fields of Learning

Ward District 7 School

Alfred School District

Alfred District 1 School

One-Room Schools: A Photographic Essay

Alfred District 2 School

Alfred District 4 School

Alfred District 5 School

Alfred District 6 School

Alfred District 7 School

Wellsville School District

Wellsville District 2 School

Wellsville District 4 School

Wellsville District 5 School

Wellsville District 6 School

Wellsville District 7 School

Wellsville District 8 School

Andover School District

Andover District 2 School

Andover District 3 School

Andover District 4 School

Andover District 5 School

Andover District 6 School

Andover District 7 School

Andover District 9 School

Fields of Learning

Willing School District

Willing District 1 School

Willing District 2 School

One-Room Schools: A Photographic Essay

Willing District 3 School

Willing District 4 School

Fields of Learning

Willing District 5 School

Independence School District

Independence District 2 School

One-Room Schools: A Photographic Essay

Independence District 3 School

Independence District 4 School

Independence District 5 School

Independence District 6 School

One-Room Schools: A Photographic Essay

Almond, Angelica, Burns Townships

Almond District 1 School

Angelica District 6 School

Burns District 1 School

CHAPTER THREE
The High Schools, 1910

At the beginning of the 20th century, a student who wanted to attend high school needed parental permission and if the student resided outside the high school attendance boundaries, was charged tuition. There were seventeen high schools in Allegany County by 1910. One-room schools could not accommodate the required high school course work and it was unlikely that the one-room school teachers had the qualifications to instruct high school subjects. There were six high schools located in separate structures from elementary or grammar schools in the following Allegany County hamlets: Allentown, Belfast, Fillmore, Rushford, Scio, and Whitesville. Eleven incorporated Allegany County villages had high schools also housed in buildings separate from elementary schools. The villages were: Alfred, Almond, Andover, Angelica, Belmont, Bolivar, Canaseraga, Cuba, Friendship, Richburg, and Wellsville. The majority of high school teachers were male and it seems that all the high school administrators were male. The high school curriculum fulfilling New York State Regents requirements offered a four-year program of instruction. Entering High School students were expected to have completed the eighth grade with evidence of a certificate and/or passing scores on Regents Examinations in Reading, Writing, Spelling, English, Arithmetic, Geography, and U. S. History with Civics.

The High School Curriculum

First Year: English, 1st year Latin or 1st year German, Algebra, Physiology and Hygiene, Drawing, biology, Ancient History.

Fields of Learning

Second Year: English, Geometry, 1st year German or 2nd year German, Caesar, English History, Drawing.

Third Year: American History, 3rd year English, Physics, 2nd year German, or Cicero, Advanced Arithmetic.

Four Year: History of Literature, Physical Geography, Commercial Geography, 4th year English.

Requirements for the *academic diploma* issued to students taking preliminary and academic examinations were: English: 13 credits, Mathematics: 10 credits, History: 10 credits, Science: 10 credits, Electives: 29 credits. The *classical academic diploma* required: English: 13 credits, Mathematics: 10 credits, History: 5 credits, Science: 5 credits, Latin: 20 credits, second foreign language: 15 credits, Electives: 4 credits. The requirements were established June 1, 1909 by the New York State Board of Education.

Credits: Language and Literature were: 1st year: 4 credits, 2nd year: 3 credits, third year: 3 credits, 4th year: 3 credits, grammar: 2 credits, History of Literature: 2 credits. Modern Languages German or French or Spanish was given 5 credits for the 1st year and 5 credits for the second year. Latin courses were awarded: Latin, 1st year: 5 credits, grammar: 1 credit, elementary composition: 1 credit, Caesar: 3 credits, Cicero: 4 credits, Advanced Composition: 1 credit, Prose at sight: 1 credit and Poetry at sight: 1 credit. In Mathematics Advanced Arithmetic earned 2 credits, Algebra received 7 credits, and Plane Geometry gained a student 5 credits. Science credits were: Biology: 5 credits or students could select two science courses from Botany: 2 ½ credits, Zoology: 2 ½ credits, or Physiology: 2 ¼ credits. In History students could take either Ancient History or English History for either 3 or 5 credits. Ancient History and Civics earned 5 credits and Economics gave a student 2 credits. Commercial Subjects earned students: Business Arithmetic: 2 credits, Bookkeeping: 4 credits, Commercial Law: 2 credits, and Business Writing: 1 credit. Commercial courses were only credited for the academic diploma. Additional subjects earning credit were: Elementary Drawing: 3 credits, Advanced Drawing: 3 credits, and Agriculture: 2 credits.

Examinations in all high school courses were standardized tests prescribed by the New York State Board of Education Regents administered at the end of the year. A *diploma* was offered based on a general average of 65. A *diploma with credit* was based on an average of 75. A *diploma with great credit* was based on an average of 85 and a *diploma with the highest credit* was based on a general average of 95. There is currently no information on what high school graduates pursued as career paths after earning their diplomas.[1] The accompanying photographs include all seventeen of Allegany County's high schools.

CHART 7

Allegany County High Schools Educational Statistics, 1916 *

Categories	Alfred	Allentown	Andover	Belfast
Enrolment	183	79	280	202
Average Attendance	145	60	220	158
Teacher Grades	College grad.: 2, College grad provisional: 2, Normal school: 3, 1st grade cert.: 1.	College grad.: 2, Normal school: 1, Training class: 1	College grad.: 2, Normal school: 3, 1st grade cert.: 3	College grad.: 3, Normal school: 5
Assessed Valuation	$281,125	$139,275	$441,939	$625,000
Expenditures	$9801.45	$5692.29	$8193.56	$19,686.63
Cost per capita	$53.56	$72.05	$29.26	$97.46
Tax Rate	$.015	$.0321	$.0133	$.0195
State Aid	$2151.48	$559.53	$1400.58	$1590.24

Categories	Belmont	Bolivar	Richburg	Scio
Enrolment	262	351	97	111
Average Attendance	207	280	81	85
Teacher Grades	College grad.: 4, Normal school: 4, 1st grade cert.: 1, special cert.: 1, training class: 1, temp. license: 1	College grad.: 4, Normal school: 3, 1st grade cert.: 1, special cert: 1	Normal School: 2, sub academic training class: 1, training class: 2	College grad.: 1, Normal school: 3, 1st grade cert.: 1, temp. license: 1
Assessed Valuation	$568,504	$641,910	$263,497	$354,996
Cost per capita	$42.48	$36.19	$45.45	$49.98
Tax Rate	$.0116	$.0133	$.0113	$.0125
State Aid	$1712.50	$1225.00	$525.00	$682.64

* Statistics for Chart 7 taken from Thomas E. Finegan's *Elementary Education Report for the School Year Ending July 31, 1916.*

Alfred High School, Alfred NY

Allentown High School, Allentown NY

The High Schools, 1910

Almond High School, Almond NY

Andover High School, Andover NY

Belfast Seminary, Belfast NY

Belmont High School, Belmont NY

The High Schools, 1910

Bolivar High School, Bolivar NY

Canaseraga High School, Canaseraga NY

Cuba High School, Cuba NY

Fillmore High School, Fillmore NY

The High Schools, 1910

Friendship High School, Friendship NY

Richburg High School, Richburg NY

Rushford Academy, Rushford NY

Scio High School, Scio NY

The High Schools, 1910

Wellsville High School, Wellsville NY

Whitesville High School, Whitesville NY

Wilsonian High School, Angelica NY

Endnotes

1	University of the State of New York. Annual Announcement and Course of Study, Allentown Union High School, Wellsville, New York: Progressive Press, 1910), no pagination.

CHAPTER FOUR
School Consolidation: K–12

Between 1910 and 1930, New York State mandated stricter enforcement of compulsory school attendance to age 16 and school consolidation with the *caveat* of increased state aid. During World War I, New York State adopted a township system of management for rural schools. The law required the establishment of a school trustee for each township, placing township schools under the management of a single board of five persons selected by the voters of the township, and a review to determine which schools were unnecessary. Further requirements stated the township would establish a uniform tax rate for school funding, rural schools would offer educational facilities at the same level as those in urban areas, and basic requirements were to be established to evaluate both the schools and the qualifications of the teachers. The law required that high schools be provided in rural areas, stricter educational training for teachers, the inclusion of a library in each school, and the expansion of the curriculum stressing the *library* and *lecture* as the tools to enlightenment. Schools were now required to enforce state laws on compulsory attendance, medical inspection laws, physical education laws, and the proper sanitation of one-room schools. New York State promoted the incorporation of *play* time as essential to foster educational development. The townships were expected to foster a community spirit and to assume the responsibility to promote education.[1]

The result was a gradual abandonment of one-room elementary schools. Consolidation demanded better trained teachers and expanded programs for sports, vocational training, and academic programs. Consolidation brought increased state funding that permitted monies for the transport of students and expanded educational programs. Consolidated schools had playgrounds, auditoriums, study rooms, vocational training for cooking classes, dressmaking, woodworking, pattern and molding classes, biology, chemistry, and physics laboratories, lunchrooms, and commercial and mechanical drawing departments.[2]

By 1945 only twenty-two one-room schools were still in use. All were closed by 1998. The collapse of both the oil industry in the 1950s and manufacturing by the beginning of the 21st century forced many Allegany County families to leave to find work. The exit of both industry and population led to a reduction of the tax base supporting education and fewer students enrolling in public schools. As a result, the county's twenty-nine townships were consolidated and now support just twelve consolidated schools' systems for grades k-to-12. Only four townships maintain their own educational plants for kindergarten to grade twelve: Andover, Scio, Whitesville (Independence), and Wellsville. The other twenty-five townships merged their school systems. Two school systems each consist of two merged townships, three school systems are the result of three townships being merged, and three school systems are the result of four townships merging.

School consolidation brought an end to separate elementary and secondary schools. All grades were included within the walls of one structure that was either an entirely new building housing K-to-12 grades or a major addition added to an existing school, usually the high school, to accommodate all thirteen grades. Wellsville Township is the exception to the pattern of all grades under one roof because as the largest village in Allegany County, the student population was too large to be housed in one building. Wellsville maintained three elementary schools. Martin Street and Hanover Street elementary schools at either end of the village were for students who could walk to school within the village borders. The original Brooklyn elementary school in the middle of Wellsville was also for walkers. A new and larger Brooklyn School was constructed in 1927 in the middle of Wellsville village for walking students and students bused from Wellsville Township and the neighboring townships of Alma and Willing as part of the consolidation process. Today, all three of Wellsville's elementary schools are merged into one elementary school in a newly constructed building. Wellsville's junior and senior high school students are housed in a structure separate from the school building accommodating elementary students.

With each merger one consolidated K-to-12 building temporarily became an elementary school while the other facility housed some K-to-6 grades and all the high school students. Costs of maintaining an older facility as just an elementary school ultimately forced their closures. As a result, many Allegany County hamlets and villages worry their identify will be lost and their population will relocate without a physical school presence. These communities fear their fate could be as tragic as Allentown, New York's when the K-to-12 school was merged with Scio Township schools in 1959. The Allentown school building was used as an elementary school until 1980 and then closed because of its age and drinking water issues. The Allentown school was sold and over several decades was seriously neglected and is currently unusable without millions of dollars in cost to rehabilitate the building. After the school's closure all of Allentown, New York's businesses gradually closed. The church and a post office are all that remain in a once thriving hamlet. Angelica, New York's residents whose school merged with Belmont necessitating the construction of a new Genesee Valley Central School have similar concerns about their village. The former Belmont Central School facility is currently unusable. The recent closure of Rushford's elementary school/former K-to-12 central school has generated the same fears about the future of its school building and whether or not Rushford will survive. Attempts to initiate the merger of Andover, Scio, and Whitesville Central Schools with neighboring school systems, has met strong community resistance. Schools anchor communities. Can communities survive without schools? The verdict is mixed.

The images below of Allentown, New York show the elementary school (white building) to the right of the high school (brick building) in 1908. The elementary school building was originally further to the left of the high school, but was moved to the location shown in the photograph to place both school facilities next to each other. In 1933, Allentown Union School expanded with a major new addition to the high school building to accommodate grades K- to -12. The original high school (the right side of the consolidated school) housed the elementary grades and the addition was for the high school grades. The Friendship School photograph shows the original high school building to the right of the expansion to accommodate all grade levels. The additional photographs show other Allegany County schools built by the 1950s to accommodate K-to-12 grades within one structure.

Allegany County in the 19th century had two religiously affiliated schools, both in Wellsville. One was associated with the Lutheran Church and the other school with the Roman Catholic Church. By the beginning of the 20th century the Lutheran school had closed. The Roman Catholic Church's Immaculate Conception School remains, but this school no longer offers a high school education ending its educational offerings with grade 8.

TABLE # 8**

TOWNSHIP SCHOOL CONSOLIDATION, ALLEGANY COUNTY, NEW YORK

Township	1869 # of one-room schools	1910 # of one-room schools	1945 # of K-12 schools	1998* # of K-12 schools
Alfred	7 + 3 joint district schools	4 + 1 high school	1	1
Allen	9 + 1 joint district schools	9	0 [i]	0
Alma	8 district schools	7 + 1 high school	1	0 [ii]
Almond	13+2 joint district schools	9 + 1 high school	1	0 [iii]
Amity	9 + 2 joint district schools	7 + 1 high school	1	1
Andover	9 + 5 joint district schools	8 + 1 high school	1	1
Angelica	7 + 2 joint district schools	5 + 1 high school	1	0 [iv]
Belfast	10+3 joint district schools	6 + 1 high school	1	1
Birdsall	6 + 3 joint district schools	6	1	0 [v]
Bolivar	6 + 3 joint district schools	7 + 1 high school	1	1
Burns	10+ 1 joint district schools	5 + 1 high school	1	1
Caneadea	13+ 1 joint district	not known	1	0 [vi]
Centerville	9 + 4 joint district schools	9	1	0 [vii]
Clarksville	7 + 4 joint district schools	7	0 [viii]	0
Cuba	12+1 joint district schools	6 + 1 high school	1	1

Page 1

TABLE # 8**

TOWNSHIP SCHOOL CONSOLIDATION, ALLEGANY COUNTY, NEW YORK

Township	1869 # of one-room schools	1910 # of one-room schools	1945 # of K-12 schools	1998* # of K-12 schools
Friendship	9 + 3 joint district schools	7 + 1 high school	1	1
Genesee	5 + 3 joint district schools	5	0[ix]	0
Granger	7 + 2 joint district schools	7	1	0[x]
Grove	8 + 2 joint district schools	9	1	0[xi]
Hume	14 district schools	12 + 1 high school	1	1
Independence	8 + 2 joint district schools	5 + 1 high school	1	1
New Hudson	12+1 joint district schools	12	0[xii]	0
Rushford	13+1 joint district schools	8 + 1 high school	1	0[xiii]
Scio	6 + 4 joint district schools	7 + 1 high school	1	1
Ward	7 + 1 joint district schools	7	0[xiv]	0
Wellsville	10+ 3 joint district schools	7 + 1 high school	1	1
West Almond	9 + 1 joint district schools	6	0[xv]	0
Willing	6 + 3 joint district schools	6	0[xvi]	0
Wirt	11+2 joint district schools	10 + 1 high school	1	0[xvii]

Page 2

Allentown, NY–1908

Allentown School, Allentown NY

Alfred—Almond Central School

Andover Central School

Angelica Central, Angelica NY

Belfast Central School

Fields of Learning

Belmont Central School

Bolivar Central School

School Consolidation: K–12

Cuba Central School, Cuba NY

Friendship Central School

Richburg Central School

Scio Central School

School Consolidation: K–12

Whitesville Central School, Whitesville NY

Martin Street School, Wellsville NY

Hanover Street School, Wellsville NY

Brooklyn Elementary School, 1897-1927

School Consolidation: K-12

Brooklyn Elementary School, 1927

Wellsville High School, Wellsville NY

Immaculate Conception School, Wellsville NY

Endnotes

1   Finnegan, Thomas E., *Elementary Education Report for the School Year Ending July 31, 1916* (Albany, New York: University of the State of New York, 1917), p. 518-524.

2   <u>Ibid</u>, p. 706-710.

i   Merged with Belfast.

ii   Merged with Scio or Wellsville.

iii   Merged with Alfred.

iv   Merged with Belmont

v   Merged with Almond/Alfred.

vi   Merged with Belfast.

vii   Merged with Fillmore (Hume).

viii   Merged with Bolivar.

ix   Merged with Bolivar.

x   Merged with Fillmore (Hume).

xi   Merged with Canaseraga (Burns).

xii   Merged with Cuba.

xiii   Merged with Cuba.

xiv   Merged with Amity or Alfred.

xv   Merged with Angelica, Almond, or Alfred.

xvi   Merged with Wellsville.

xvii   Merged with Bolivar.

*   In 2019 there are only 12 schools with grades K-12 remaining for Allegany County, New York's 29 townships: Alfred, Amity (Belmont and Angelica), Andover, Belfast, Bolivar-Richburg, Burns (Canaseraga), Cuba, Friendship, Hume (Filmore), Independence (Whitesville), Scio, and Wellsville.

**   Statistics for this chart are distributed throughout the book by Thomas E. Finegan, *Elementary Education Report for the School Year Ending July 31, 1916*.

CHAPTER FIVE
Higher Education in Allegany County

Following behind the migrating New Englanders who entered and settled Allegany County were various religious groups seeking to find converts as they spread the word of God. Two religious groups who settled in Allegany County founded institutions of higher learning. *Seventh Day Baptists* founded Alfred University in eastern Allegany County in 1836. Alfred University was established as a non-sectarian institution open to women, African-Americans, and Native-Americans in Alfred, New York, a village named for the legendary King Alfred. The second institution of higher learning was Houghton College in northern Allegany County. This college was founded in 1883 by the *Wesleyan Methodist Church* and was named for Wesleyan minister, Willard J. Houghton. Houghton College has always been a religiously affiliated institution training students for the ministry.

In 1908, then Alfred University President, Boothe C. Davis, persuaded the New York State Legislature to locate the New York State School of Agriculture at the Alfred University Campus. In 1941, the School of Agriculture was granted Junior College status and renamed the New York State Agricultural and Technical College of Alfred with campuses in both Alfred and Wellsville, New York.

Alfred University Buildings in Alfred NY

Higher Education in Allegany County

Aerial View of Houghton College, Genesee County Houghton, NY

CHAPTER SIX
Surviving One-Room Schools: 2019

Each township's one-room schools were given a number. However, as new one-room schools were built and other one-room schools were closed, the numbers were changed making it difficult to trace each structure's history by a designated township number. After closure one-room schools were put up for sale. Some were never sold and over time abandoned and/or razed. Sold or donated one-room schools were converted into businesses, churches, libraries, and museums. The majority in Allegany County became either full-time or seasonal residences.

Two of the greatest success stories in recycling one-room schools is in Genesee Township in Allegany County. District 1 School in Little Genesee is the second school on this site with multiple rooms to accommodate the hamlet's growing student population. It replaced the one-room school that burned in 1901. The new District School I in Little Genesee was an example of mass vernacular school architecture with an impressive bell tower centered above the main door. Today, minus the bell tower, District 1 School is a beautifully maintained library for Genesee Township.

Genesee Township District 6 School is in Ceres, New York. This building, an example of folk vernacular architecture, was more than one room but only one story. Falling on hard times, the building was rescued by the BRAG (Bolivar, Richburg, Allentown, and Genesee) Historical Society with the support of Jean Milliman, Genesee Township Historian. Under Jean's leadership BRAG purchased the building, raised the funds to rehabilitate the structure, and opened the school as a museum for BRAG exhibitions. Jean Milliman's tireless efforts got the Ceres School placed on the National Register of Historic Places by the Department of the Interior of the United States in 2010.

A third excellent example of a re-purposed rural school is the Alfred Township District 1 School. It currently houses a United States Post Office and was expanded to include a fire station.

Chart # 9

Surviving One-Room Schools

Township	Residence	Cabin	Abandoned	Razed	Other
Alfred	4				1: Post Office & Fire Dept. 1: Bicycle Shop
Allen	3	1	2	1	
Alma	2		2		
Almond	5				1: Grange
Amity	4		1		
Andover	2		1		
Angelica	3	2			
Belfast	4	1			1: barn
Birdsall					
Bolivar	1		1		2: Churches
Burns	3				
Caneadea	3	1			
Centerville	3	1	2		
Clarksville	4		1		
Cuba	5	1			
Friendship	2		1		
Genesee	1	1			1: Library 1: Museum
Granger	3				
Grove	2				1: Church
Hume	8		2		1: Museum 1: Unknown
Independence	2				
New Hudson	4		2	1	1: barn 1: garage 1: storage
Rushford	6	1			2: garage 1: barn
Scio	1	1			
Wellsville	5				
West Almond	5				
Willing	2				1: Church
Wirt					

Allegany County Township Historians have been able to document what happened to many, but not all, of the one-room schools in their townships. The chart below is not a complete list but offers a record about the fate of many of these schools. No information could be found for Birdsall and Wirt townships. The accompanying photographs offer current views of some of Allegany County's one-room schools.

Alfred District 1 School | Post Office and Fire Station

Genesee District 6 School, Ceres NY | *BRAG Museum Sign*

Genesee District 6 School, Ceres NY | *BRAG Museum*

Alfred District 2 School | Business

Alma District 1 School | Residence

Alma District 2 School | Abandoned

Alma District 5 School | Residence

Almond District 1 School | Garage

Andover District 1 School | Residence

Bolivar District 4 School | Abandoned

Bolivar District 5 School | Church

Bolivar District 6 School | Church

Cuba District 6 School | Residence

Genesee District 1 School | Library

Grove District 6 School | Church

Hume District 4 School | Town of Hume Museum

Hume District 8 School | Abandoned

Hume District 14 School | Use Unknown

New Hudson District 8 School | Abandoned

Rushford District 10 School | Residence

Willing District 8 School | Community Center

ART AND PHOTOGRAPHIC CREDITS

Cover Art

Fields of Learning, watercolor by David A. Dean with the artist's permission.

Chapter One

One-Room Schools in Allegany County, New York: A History: images courtesy of the Allegany County Historical Society and Museum, Andover, New York.

Chapter Two

One-Room Schools in Allegany County, New York: A Photographic Essay: images courtesy of the Allegany County Historical Society and Museum, Andover, New York.

Chapter Three

The High Schools, 1910: Fillmore High School, courtesy of the Allegany County Historical Society and Museum, Andover, New York. All other photographs are from the collection of Dr. William Paquette.

Chapter Four

Consolidation: K-to-12:Angelica Central School, Friendship Central School, Richburg Central School, Whitesville Central School, Brooklyn Elementary School 1897-1927, and Brooklyn Elementary School, 1927, are courtesy of the Allegany County Historical Society and Museum,

Andover, New York. All other photographs are from the collection of Dr. William Paquette.

Chapter Five

Higher Education: Images are from the collection of Dr. William Paquette.

Chapter Six

One-Room Schools: 2019: Alma District 2, Alma District 5, Almond District 1, Bolivar District 5, Bolivar District 6, Genesee District 1, Genesee District 6 (two images) are from the collection of Dr. William Paquette. All other images are courtesy of the Allegany County Historical Society and Museum, Andover, New York.

BIBLIOGRAPHY

Allentown Union High School, 1909-1910. Wellsville, NY: Progressive Press, 1910.

Angelica Sesquicentennial Historical and Memorial, 1805-1955. Sesquicentennial Committee, 1955.

Beers, F.W. *History of Allegany County, New York 1806-1879.* New York: F.W. Beers & Co., 1879.

Beers, F.W. *Insurance Maps of Allegany County, New York.* New York: F.W. Beers & Co., 1869.

Browne, Ray B. and Marshall Fishwick. *Icons of America.* Bowling Green, OH: Bowling Green University Press, 1978.

Cuba, Incorporated as a Village for a Century, 1859-1950. Cuba, NY: Cuba Centennial Committee, 1950.

Cyr, Frank W. and Henry H. Linn. *Planning Rural Community School Buildings.* NY: Teachers College Press Columbia University, 1949.

The Derrick, Allentown High School, 1933. Self-published.

Finegan, Thomas E. *Elementary Education, Report for the School Year Ending July 31, 1916.*
Albany, NY: University of the State of New York, 1917.

Fuller, Wayne E. *One-Room Schools of the Middle West.* Lawrence, Kansas: University Press of Kansas, 1994.

Gentle Slopes and Homespun Folks, Town of Genesse Sesquicentennial, 1830-1980. Town of Genesee Book Committee, 1980.

Gilbert, Helen J. White. *Rushford and Rushford People.* Chautauqua Print Shop, 1910.

Gulliford, Andrew. *America's Country Schools.* Washington, DC: The Preservation press, 1984.

Herzog, Mary Jean Ronan and Robert B. Pittman. "Home, Family, and Community, Ingredients in the Rural Education Equation." *Phi Delta Kappan.* October, 1995, 113+.

Howe, Martha Elston. *A History of the Town of Wellsville, New York.* Wellsville, NY: By Author, 1963.

Jackson, John Brinckerhoff. *Discovering the Vernacular Landscape.* New Haven: Yale University Press, 1984.

Minard, John S. *Allegany County and its People.* Alfred, New York: W.A. Fergusson & Co., 1896.

Minard, John S. *The Log School House Period.* Cuba, NY: Free Press, 1905.

Newman, Lucille Thornton. *History of Angelica, New York.* 1970.

Paquette, William. *The Root Family of Bolivar, New York*. Baltimore: Gateway Press, 1991.

Schroeder, Fred. "Educational Legacy: Rural One Room School house." *Historic Preservation*, July/September 1997, 4+.

Schroeder, Fred. "Schoolhouse Reading: What You can Learn from your Rural School." *History News*, Vol. 36, 1981, 4+.

Scio Sesquicentennial, Scio, NY 1823-1973. Scio Sesquicentennial Committee, 1973.

Sesquicentennial, A Collected History of a Town and Its People, Town of Amity, 1830-1980. Belmont, NY: Amity Press, 1980.

Sesquicentennial History of Whitesville, NY, 1821-1971. Westfield, PA: Valley Dollar Saver, 1971.

Shear, Hazel M. *The Wellsville Story, The Willing Story, The Alma Story*. Wellsville, NY: Benson Smythe Publishers, 1997.

Sloane, Eric. *The Little Red Schoolhouse*. Garden City, NY: Doubleday & Co., Inc., 1972.

Town of Bolivar, New York Sesquicentennial 1825-1975. Bolivar, NY: The Committee, 1975.

About the Contributors

David A. Dean. Dave Dean is a lifelong Allegany County resident. He attended Allentown Union School, Wellsville Central School, and Scio Central School where he graduated. Dave began painting in 1987 after shoulder surgery for something to do. He has always been interested in architecture and architectural design and his paintings reflect his love of antiquated buildings. Dave Dean enjoys the interpretations his paintings inspire when he talks to potential buyers. He feels that people enjoying his art is the best critique. Dave Dean resides at 1181 White Hill Road, Bolivar, New York 14715. His website is: www.artbydavedean.com and Dave can be reached at bumpadino.yahoo.com or at 585-593-1028.

Allegany County Historical Society. The Allegany Historical Society was formed December 17, 1971 and went dormant in 1976. The Society was revived April 20, 2010 with Ron Taylor as its first President serving from 2010 to 2011. Ron Taylor was reelected President in 2017, 2018, and 2019. The Allegany Historical Society and Museum in Andover, New York opened January 14, 2017 and is located at 11 East Greenwood Street. Ron Taylor was selected as the Museum's first Executive Director. Ron Taylor has been collecting photographs of Allegany County's one-room schools since the 1970s and in 2010 and 2011 encouraged all the township historians to photograph their surviving schools. Ron Taylor is a graduate of Allentown Union School.

William A. Paquette, Ph. D. (United States) was a Professor of History at Tidewater Community College in Portsmouth, Virginia where he taught Latin American History, World Civilization, U. S. History, and

Western Civilization. Professor Paquette received a Master's Degree from Duquesne University (Pittsburgh) and a Ph. D. from Emory University (Atlanta). During his academic career, Dr. Paquette was awarded 14 National Endowment for the Humanities Grants for professional study and Institutional grants that enabled him to study and conduct research in China and Japan. He traveled to southern Mexico over a ten-year period examining the archaeology at Maya and Aztec sites and studied the Maya language at Duke University (Durham, NC). Professor Paquette presented research at international conferences at the University of Louvain (Belgium), the Sorbonne (Paris), the University of Acala de Henares (Spain), the University of Copenhagen (Denmark), Lorand Eotvos University (Budapest), and San Pablo University (Madrid). He has published over 165 articles and thirteen books and served as a consultant to the U.S. Department of Education, the United States Institute of Peace, the National Endowment for the Humanities, and all major history textbook publishers. For a decade, he was the History Editor for the international MERLOT (Multimedia Education Resources for Learning and Online Teaching) Project instructing college and university faculty on how to teach online courses. Dr. Paquette was annually listed in *Who's Who in America* and *Who's Who in the World*. During his professional career Dr. Paquette met the late King Michael I and the late Queen Anne of Romania, King Simeon II of Bulgaria, the late Pope John Paul II, the Dalai Lama, members of the British Royal Family, and numerous Heads of Government from European States. Dr. Paquette attended Allentown Union School for grades kindergarten to six, Scio Central School for part of grade 7, and Wellsville High School for grades 7 to 12.

www.ingramcontent.com/pod-product-compliance
Lightning Source LLC
Chambersburg PA
CBHW052037070526
44584CB00016B/2075